U.S. Government Q&A!

What Is a CONSTITUTIONAL Amendment?

By Theresa Emminizer

Gareth Stevens PUBLISHING

Please visit our website, www.garethstevens.com. For a free color catalog of all our high-quality books, call toll free 1-800-542-2595 or fax 1-877-542-2596.

Library of Congress Cataloging-in-Publication Data
Names: Emminizer, Theresa, author.
Title: What is a Constitutional Amendment? / Theresa Emminizer.
Description: Buffalo : Gareth Stevens Publishing, 2026. | Series: U.S. government Q & A! | Includes index. | Audience: Grades 2-3
Identifiers: LCCN 2024045549 (print) | LCCN 2024045550 (ebook) | ISBN 9781482470086 (library binding) | ISBN 9781482470079 (paperback) | ISBN 9781482470093 (ebook)
Subjects: LCSH: Constitutional amendments–United States–Juvenile literature. | Constitutional law–United States–Juvenile literature.
Classification: LCC KF4555 .E46 2026 (print) | LCC KF4555 (ebook) | DDC 342.7303–dc23/eng/20241029
LC record available at https://lccn.loc.gov/2024045549
LC ebook record available at https://lccn.loc.gov/2024045550

First Edition

Published in 2026 by
Gareth Stevens Publishing
2544 Clinton Street
Buffalo, NY 14224

Designer: Andrea Davison-Bartolotta
Editor: Kristen Nelson

Photo credits: Cover, pp. 1, 15 Everett Collection/Shutterstock.com; series art (paper, feather) Incomible/Shutterstock.com; series art (blue banner, red banner, stars) pingbat/Shutterstock.com; p. 5 File:Scene at the Signing of the Constitution of the United States.jpg/Wikimedia Commons; p. 7 mark reinstein/Shutterstock.com; p. 9 Visitor7/File:Bill of Rights Memorial-1.jpg/Wikimedia Commons; p. 11 Joseph Sohm/Shutterstock.com; pp. 13, 14, 19 courtesy of Library of Congress; p. 16 Ken Wolter/Shutterstock.com; p. 17 Rob Crandall/Shutterstock.com.

Printed in the United States of America

CPSIA compliance information: Batch #CSGS26: For further information contact Gareth Stevens, New York, New York at 1-800-542-2595.

Contents

Words in the glossary appear in **bold** type the first time they are used in the text.

A Living Document

The U.S. Constitution is the set of laws by which America is governed. Written in 1787, the U.S. Constitution is the oldest written national constitution that's still in use today! The Constitution is a living document. That means it's meant to change over time to better meet the needs of the people.

A constitutional amendment is a change or addition to the Constitution. More than 11,000 amendments have been introduced, or presented, in Congress! Only 27 amendments have been approved, or passed.

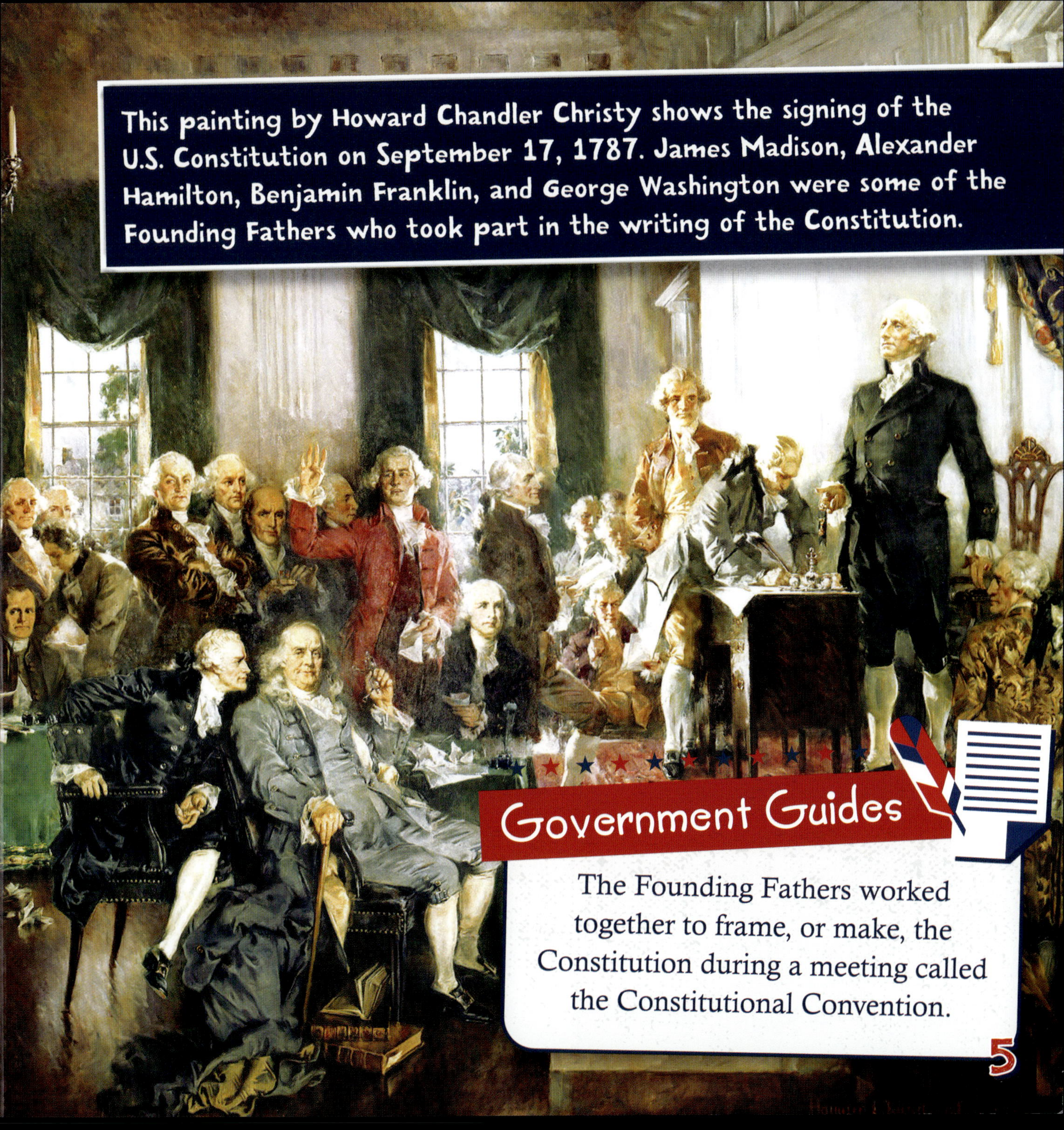

This painting by Howard Chandler Christy shows the signing of the U.S. Constitution on September 17, 1787. James Madison, Alexander Hamilton, Benjamin Franklin, and George Washington were some of the Founding Fathers who took part in the writing of the Constitution.

Government Guides

The Founding Fathers worked together to frame, or make, the Constitution during a meeting called the Constitutional Convention.

The Amendment Process

Passing a constitutional amendment isn't easy. A lot of people need to agree that it's the right thing to do!

First, an amendment is proposed in Congress. The Senate and House of **Representatives** vote on it. A two-thirds majority is needed for the amendment to move on to the next step. Then, three-fourths of state legislatures must approve the amendment. Or, states may hold conventions to vote on the amendment. It still needs three-fourths of these conventions to vote in favor of it to pass.

Government Guides

Another way amendments may be proposed is if two-thirds of state legislatures call for a constitutional convention. However, this has never been done.

Some constitutional amendments are proposed, or suggested, to change how the government works. Some are about people's rights and freedoms. Most amendment proposals never leave Congress, shown here.

The Bill of Rights

The first 10 constitutional amendments **protect** the individual rights of Americans. They also check the power of the government. These 10 amendments, **ratified** December 15, 1791, are collectively called the Bill of Rights.

The First Amendment of the Bill of Rights **guarantees** freedom of speech, press, and religion, or faith, among other rights. Other amendments cover how people should be treated if they are thought to have committed, or done, a crime. The Bill of Rights also protects Americans from unreasonable searches and fines, and more.

Government Guides

The Ninth Amendment says that Americans also have more rights that aren't listed in the Constitution.

The Bill of Rights Monument in Phoenix, Arizona, honors the lasting importance of the Bill of Rights.

States' Rights

States' rights were a key issue, or problem, among the Founding Fathers who wrote the Constitution. So, the 10th Amendment was included in the Bill of Rights. It gives powers not listed in the Constitution to the states. This has been **interpreted** many ways in U.S. history.

The 11th amendment established, or set up, state sovereign immunity. That means if someone wishes to bring a lawsuit against the state they live in, they must do it in a state court.

Government Guides

Thomas Jefferson was one of the Founding Fathers who strongly supported states' rights.

Even today, each state has its own flag and constitution.

The 13th, 14th, and 15th Amendments

The 13th Amendment passed in 1865. It abolished, or outlawed, slavery in the United States. In 1868, the 14th Amendment granted, or gave, **citizenship** to all people born in the United States. The 15th Amendment stated that a male citizen's right to vote couldn't be denied, or blocked, based on race, color, or having been **enslaved** in the past.

These amendments took the first steps toward civil rights for all. Still, states found ways to continue to **oppress** people of color for a long time.

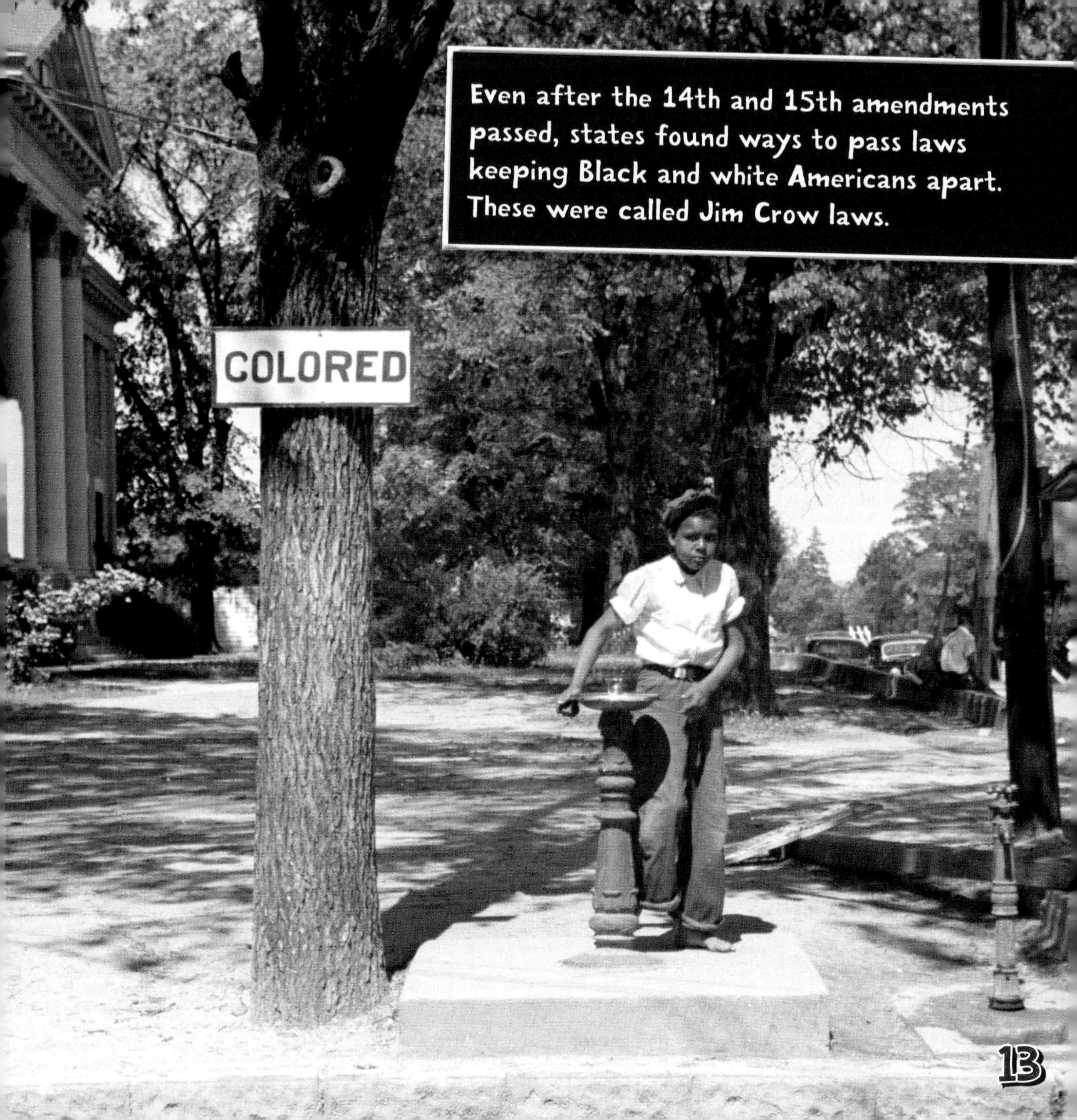

Even after the 14th and 15th amendments passed, states found ways to pass laws keeping Black and white Americans apart. These were called Jim Crow laws.

Women's Suffrage

The 14th and 15th Amendments gave the right to vote to all male citizens over age 21. But, until a constitutional amendment passed, woman weren't guaranteed the right to vote across the United States. Many people who fought against slavery also hoped to win suffrage, or the right to vote, for all citizens.

An amendment for women's suffrage was first introduced in Congress in 1878. It took years, but the 19th Amendment was ratified in 1920. It said American women had the right to vote!

women's suffrage march, Washington, DC, 1913

Government Guides

Women's suffragist Susan B. Anthony once said: "It was we, the people; not we, the white male citizens; nor yet we, the male citizens; but we, the whole people, who formed the Union."

Women did have voting rights in some parts of the United States before the 19th Amendment passed, but these rights were limited.

Other Key Changes

Other amendments have to do with how representatives such as the president, vice president, and senators are elected. In 1951, the 22nd Amendment placed a limit on presidential terms of office. It says presidents can only serve two terms.

The 25th amendment states that the vice president takes on the presidency if the president dies, steps down, or is removed from office. It also gives rules for what to do if the president is very sick or unable to do their duties for a time.

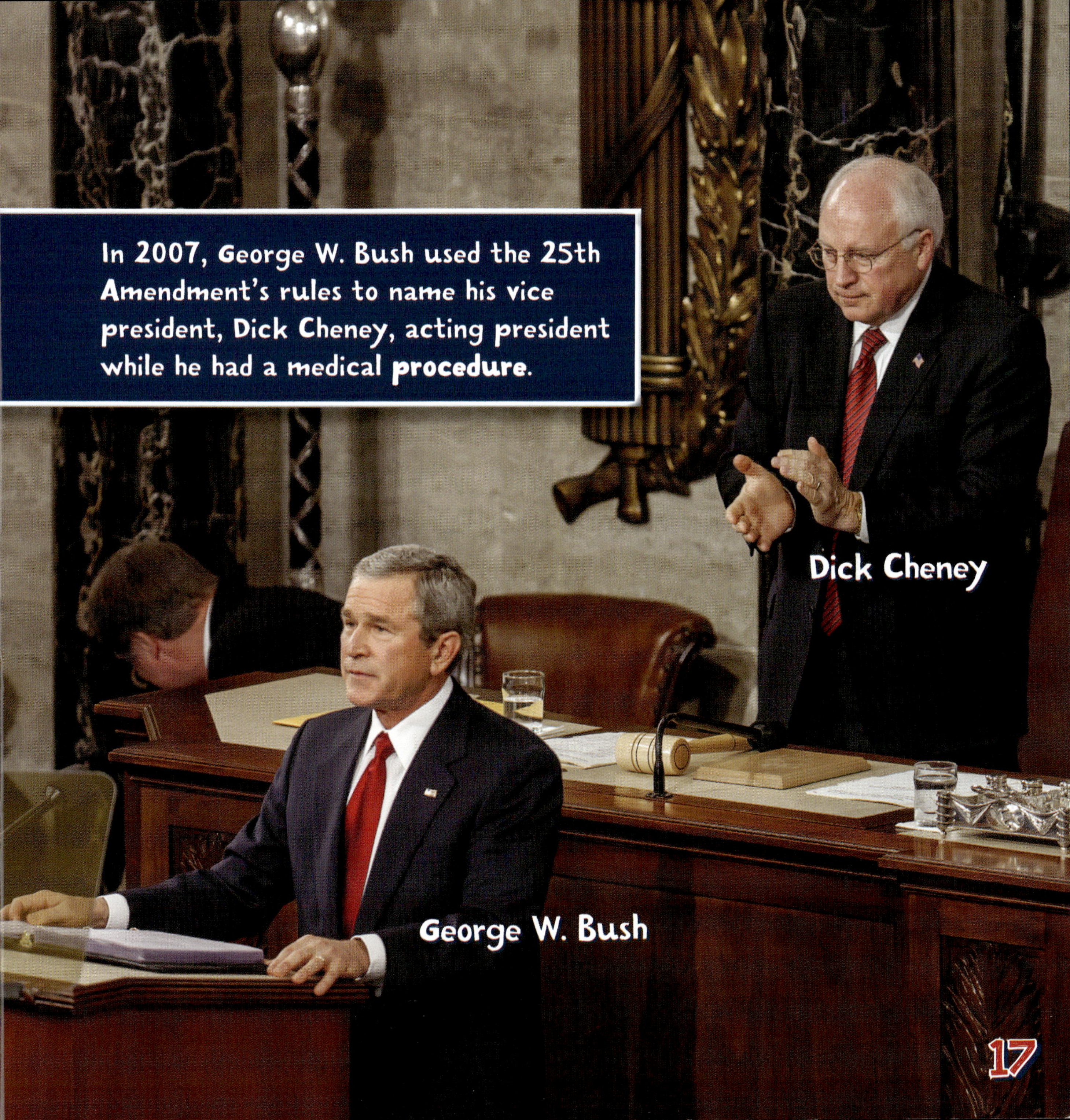
In 2007, George W. Bush used the 25th Amendment's rules to name his vice president, Dick Cheney, acting president while he had a medical **procedure**.
Dick Cheney
George W. Bush

Repealing an Amendment

Repealing an amendment means overturning it. Only one constitutional amendment has been repealed so far. It was repealed by the passage of another amendment!

The 18th Amendment of 1919 is sometimes called the Prohibition amendment. It was about prohibiting, or making illegal, the sale of alcohol in the United States. The 21st Amendment, which was ratified in 1933, repealed the 18th Amendment. The 21st Amendment also granted greater power to state governments, allowing them to make their own laws about alcohol regulation, or control.

This photo shows a member of the New York City Police overseeing alcohol being thrown away during Prohibition. Alcohol is a clear liquid that's in drinks such as wine and beer that can make a person think and respond slowly, or act differently than they normally would.

What's Next?

Although it was written more than 230 years ago, in many ways the Constitution of the United States has grown and changed alongside the country. Constitutional amendments are written to make the Constitution better as the needs of the American people become clearer.

Many of these amendments were hard won. **Abolitionists**, suffragists, and other civil rights activists fought long battles to change people's minds about the way things had been done historically. What amendments might come next?

Think About It!

Think about life in America today. What would you suggest as the next constitutional amendment? Are there any amendments you think should be repealed?

Passing an Amendment

1

An amendment is proposed by Congress. Two-thirds of the House and Senate vote in favor of it.

The amendment goes to state legislatures, or state conventions are held.

The amendment is ratified if three-quarters of state legislatures vote in favor of it, or three-quarters of state conventions vote in favor of it.

2

Two-thirds of state legislatures ask for a constitutional convention.

Congress calls the convention.

States send representatives to the convention. Amendments are proposed.

An amendment is agreed to at the convention.

The amendment is ratified by three-fourths of state legislatures or state conventions.

There are two ways an amendment can be passed, but the first way is the only way that's been used in U.S. history.

Glossary

abolitionist: One who fights to end slavery.

citizenship: Having to do with being a citizen, or a person who has all the rights and protections offered by a government.

enslaved: Having to do with being owned by another person and forced to work without pay.

guarantee: Promise.

interpret: To explain something's meaning or to understand something in a certain way.

oppress: To use power unjustly over another. Also, treating people in a cruel or unfair way.

procedure: An operation or other medical treatment.

protect: To keep safe. Protection is the act of shielding from harm.

ratify: To give formal approval to something.

representative: A member of a lawmaking body who acts for voters.

For More Information

Books

Schaefer, Benjamin Mark. *What Are States' Rights?* New York, NY: Gareth Stevens Publishing, 2022.

Silva, Sadie. *The U.S. Constitution*. Buffalo, NY: Cavendish Square Publishing, 2022.

Walton, Kathryn. *The Bill of Rights*. Buffalo, NY: Enslow Publishing, 2024.

Websites

Bill of Rights
https://bensguide.gpo.gov/bill-of-rights-1789-91
Find out more about the first 10 amendments of the Constitution, the Bill of Rights.

National Archives
www.archives.gov/founding-docs/bill-of-rights/what-does-it-say
Find out more about the Bill of Rights in this detailed exploration of the first 10 amendments.

National Constitution Center
constitutioncenter.org/the-constitution/amendments
Discover more about the 27 constitutional amendments.

Publisher's note to educators and parents: Our editors have carefully reviewed these websites to ensure that they are suitable for students. Many websites change frequently, however, and we cannot guarantee that a site's future contents will continue to meet our high standards of quality and educational value. Be advised that students should be closely supervised whenever they access the internet.

Index